THE GREATEST FILMS

THE GREATEST FILMS

A POEM

FAIZAL DEEN

MAWENZI
HOUSE

We acknowledge the support of the Canada Council for the Arts for our publishing program. We also acknowledge support from the Government of Ontario through the Ontario Arts Council.

 ONTARIO ARTS COUNCIL
CONSEIL DES ARTS DE L'ONTARIO
an Ontario government agency
un organisme du gouvernement de l'Ontario

 Canada Council Conseil des arts
for the Arts du Canada

Cover art by Ramona Ramlochand

Cover design by Sabrina Pignataro

Library and Archives Canada Cataloguing in Publication

Deen, Faizal, 1968-, author
    The greatest films / Faizal Deen.

Poems.

ISBN 978-1-927494-83-7 (paperback)

    I. Title.

PS8557.E295G74 2016   C811'.54   C2016-904660-5

Printed and bound in Canada by Coach House Printing

Mawenzi House Publishers Ltd.
39 Woburn Avenue (B)
Toronto, Ontario M5M 1K5
Canada
www.mawenzihouse.com

For the Astor, Globe, Metropole, Plaza,
& Strand cinemas of Guyana of
the 1970s.

And for my big sisters, who still take
me to the movies.

Contents

MOM & BOB: Matinees

*

Pink man turkey neck & Mom never brings home doggie bags.
that's Demico chicken in a basket, take away twinkle eyes,
Mom don't forget
no negro Indian whiteman in the veins. or how Funk Wagnalls
does Caucasian cha cha cha. So: Mom brings Bob home in the dark.

*

Bob from Manitoba, somewhere near Brandon; he'n Bartica
made snake eyes together.
"73, 732 sq. m. in W. Canada," the Assiniboine speaks
& when Mom comes back she doesn't bring
scraps; but she has plenty of left-over bones
from the mooneye she kill.

*

"Manitoba," Funk & Wagnalls says, "not Magyar. Aryan
Anglo-Saxon. not Breton race-stocks."
& when Bob asks, "who is she?" who is Mom? Uncle Sultan says,
"my sister will never any whiteman capital Winnipeg touch.
she fancy Mr Rochester country
where the animals have faces so many damn right!"

*

when the Liberty opens in Old Spice, Mom & Bob in balcony
all alone no chaperone & no Asha Bhosle
flickers let's misbehave
Brando & pit erupts "scunt!" bottles flung
at the screen: poomb!

Mom & Bob eyes shut in this dernière tango Paris derrière
wish they could throw the Parigi story at the screen
get married move to Ottawa
but dead Brando hurts the eyes to read this English
in Anchor butter
bend the pirouettes at the end
this right wrong show that flickers, hold on!
fellatio fedoras the film because!

*

a high-noon, bug-out unhappy endings kids we don't know,
Guyana izzan island Gary Cooper must win? no?
listen kids Uncle Sultan yells, "& does piss & white rum
coming up on you?"
cutaway Sacred Heart me behind Sister Brian nodding off at 11 a.m.
Mom at Palm Court Main Street with Uncle Sultan.
Georgetown to Timehri to Madiwini trucking shots
& no anaconda passing traffic.

*

Cheddi Jagan next door squeezing a post-stroke rubber ball
on the terrace is a boom shot &
The Merrymen in from Barbados & the rule of nouns I've learned
from Mom & Bob
& Bob smells Lucky Luke-like.

*

Mom: "I don't want another white rum coolieman, 'Another one,
bhai! Another one!' pissing his pants."
of course, this is only a matinee.
no late shows, pictures without sound. "How do they go? The
songs?" I ask.

*

a kiss made the red man red, I think Mom has jugs like all the men
will one day look at me.

I sing "Chaiyya re chaiyya re" through recess, through lunch
room
scholar me

too much world cinema, that radio there, a ceiling fan, hooves
running in the yard
next door, hear?

when 20,000 leagues dissolves into the flickers.

BOYHOOD THINKS: Outside Foreign

last boy stands.
       Gibralter.
the vaak villain junk mash-up coolie screams, "Put your helmets on!"
did you wake up the scientist for me? where will I touch ground?
approximately.
on TV
they say: the Nubian desert.

grab Atlas laugh through the jib shots
hurtle down from space without Sentry System sissy
red Sandals Grande Antigua alert
that's quite a crater, eh?
what Indu sadhu leaves rifle barrel at bullet speed?
       remember?
Bharati? Avadhi? Bihari?

smashing glass in the underpass Dollar Bills Alternative Tuesdays
really gay.

on TV
they say: the Nubian desert,
though no one says it like that, least not in Kingston, Ontario, 1988
before Grandpa dies *joins the car crash set*
Mom to Georgetown toothpaste 140 Guyanese dollars.

learned a new word today *Rajastaniatombomb.*
"in the shape of an ibex with wheels" steaming up the night rooms
Canada izzan island
a soju zombie in Jongno. a burnished book, Yooshij, poet
stolen from Grandpa. me,

a retreating sign from Gilan.
>not Ghana. Guyana.

In Hyoung says, "The Japanese turned Changgyeong into a zoo."

Thursday night fights in Alta Vista, a family tree is a house.
Billings Bridge Bus (#148) scattered Guyanese Labour Day
weekend Scarborough ole higue auntie
memorize April showers! tonight spring fights birds bees
my Tony Leung blue waterfall
wet dreams.
Caetano laughs out his stitches
sheds skin as Champlain chomps into Linden Forbes
jerked off rain a few blocks away
sketch Arawaks along the Rideau River
their roadside minarets tall in hollyhocks.

>remember?
there is no masjid on Arch Street.
on TV.
& Grandpa's house sharpens knives against your mangled pyla
kalma twya,

>>>cut auntieman out,
nightmares scout Ray Harryhausen blanket hippogriff mister
hides the marzipan from his witching hour sweet tooth
I shoot my orchestra in hoarse Sydney Sheldon.

Grandpa knows I spill my beans in *outside* discos.

>Gibralter.
on TV, foreign,
they say: the Nubian desert.
alligators awake la petite mort
I squander my white hotels

Bellies upright,
        ABCs photographable love.
                  in the morning,
ajoshi sweeps up the used rubbers
serviced by rainstorms this morning all I want is a Western
breakfast
get cracking ice
spring sinks.

MUSEUM: Fish Eyes

jungle
coughs
jumbie
sucks
blood
chews
sheds
skin

                                you know it as Hajee soul, massa
see Ba'ap in strange feathers on the sam
Amazon masquerami
commonpoor continental nanny wine down so
laughs past midnight
                                no, i know, Guyana izzan island

colossal afternoon pang. i make matinees. drippy features.
Bob by the Demerara.
all that white-man-gone-primitive shit. shuffleboard, sweets.
Mom. dessert fork. right hand.
praemonēre we'd crawl out've portholes, die again 6th Form
Latin ocean.

Bob said: "Go ahead. Try the custard."
more Coke bottles lost in that photo. bury fish rhymes in a kiss.
lazy eyes.
blue eye bottle neck bye bye bushy mouth.

tonight,
don't dream
crowded mind horns
where ears sing
less than Greek
little weak
open
speak.

WAR CRIMINALS: Recherché

i am in an ocean in an oven

and the white boys drink Pelasgians in Libya
bring Ovid lustier than connect the dots Wolfe Island
a plaid laugh in Madras underlined in pencil
grow the kind kids make and leave on dinner tables
hearts eyes of Mom so many streets of Billy
a piss a toke a feast of warm coke as the Neapolitan drips

return to find Archie's geography click clack Port Sprainers
windy drive home to Westmoorings stickball doubles *oye como va*
sated Spanish pencils rubbers
Flipflash islands 20th Century acetate
family portrait by dead Archie dead ab we never said *father*

he drove a Mercury strong-nose Amru al-Qays.

Dear Billy,
In Tobago, my tongue still spews Smokey & Bunty's in St James.
I see the Rafeek Mosque drive in from Piarco.
Of course, I had to write a calypso.
Not a naughty one. Everyone knows big bamboo.
Or, a newspaper one: Adolf Hitler
get kick red, hot & blue: feet taps floor
finger drums table everywhere
> *love turn the fallen*
> *anaconda back*
> *my Cuffy up top*
> *Cuffy anaconda back on the back*
> *surprise parade of parrot fish*
> *eyelash wink*
> *send him back*
> *blink blue essequibo love*
> *turn anaconda back*
> *to you Henri-Julien -27*
> *Guyana izzan island on*
> *BBC Weather*

Deleted Scene

~~Archie my father now stuck in mannerist frames~~
~~on a mantle above a fire I don't keep me warm~~
~~like the poet says, it's pornography up there~~
~~look at him join the dead ones lined up on Christmas morning~~
~~on this coast Heart of the Amazon don't ask don't see, but~~
~~it's OK to sing a bit in the morning~~
~~the deal he makes with me~~
~~him in story cotton wool tree~~
~~presents from Guyana Stores~~
~~kerchief.~~

~~Mom & Archie's trick to equal night and day beat beat shadows~~
~~Kernel Wilde in The Naked Prey~~
~~With Mom, I hunt Archie~~
~~why? he die too far across the sand~~

~~he dies, darling, beneath the moon~~

~~under the sun I sit atop Archie~~

~~adoptee~~

WAR CRIMINALS: La Boîte Noire

45 years all the ears listen for Tarantula!
Later, Barbara Streisand *I went down to the demonstration*
to get my fair share of abuse.
Flashbacks by Inigo Jones. Lisgar Street rabbit warren.
Mom in one cube, Bob in the other.
In Canada, palm end porno speeds up free of Archie's death play.
A marble façade foyer rises in space.
I wear white like Horatio. Brando's lusty back. In Mellors,
Alec Scudder parlor smoke whorehouse
music & prayers I can't pronounce. bizmAllah?
hiruvman? niraheem?
Eid-ie sweet tooth money. Sunday kites praying
fathers Camel Walk into a world of marvels. Doug McClure's lips.
Dinosaurs. Gods.
Lost national geographicals in Mowsie teeth. Snow cone
National Park.
I surrender the last metro to broken down folks.
Au Revoir Amerindia. Bacchic disco, Proust in innocent Spring.
Rough in age,
red rocket smashing moons in Spain.
Steve McQueen mamas barbed-wire border sings
oh Someone To Watch Over Me.
Edgar Rice woolly rhino burrows in pop! Thomas Kisbees.
Poseidon bulwark. Gunwale.
Shelly Winters hangs from a chandelier.
Canada izzan Omar Sharif tamarind island.
mangled Maureen McGovern rolling sea.
Fuck you to the morning after there's got to be.
Vorspiel, Godspell, rain?
I'm curious, Billy.

Mr Perel. Zipper factory. The 7th day snip. Frenulem Fitra.
Fuck off!
I remember The Alamo.

MUSEUM: Drive-in

star gazing expired father lost in me
debris of mirrors

ornate
fret
work

on fascia boards and windowsills

mid-afternoon oh fuck there he is he can't even wait for the night

Archie
grabs
oily
poulouries

Köppen
throws up ocean

don't
scorn
Efreeti
the voyage across

Two-storey wooden house with enclosed bottom flat and open front
stairs entering
the gallery in its centre with gable end roof design features

boy
school
high
Prospero
book

                                                drown
                                                  get
                                                 sunk

my father was a Fullahman.

BOYHOOD THINKS: Fazlah Découpage

Sticky.
Weewee I not wake not in up.

sci-fi Fukishima tangles up sons as Elizabeth Taylor chooses
this time to die with no anthems.
waterspout daughters turn up the TV.
India gets study in books left in cafés beside melted cakes.

approaching pavonis mons by balloon we hear mazurkas
with coffee again again a true night of Minnie Ripperton

bump grind Bob smells sex everywhere in the jump up.

mind flames fires up the archipelago stops at St Lucia,
no aunties there.

awake Ottawa into plantation dream,
press into broken morning bread   tell me in
Guyanese.

Khatoon's clockwork orchid blooms above sweaty suitcases
before Canada
Bob's 3-prong country.
                    Tell me

walk around the block Zombie on repeat empire of piss rivers
far out pharouch instead of pow! I bang the drum acapella cluster
bomb buy L'île Noire in English
Bob said downtown Ottawa looks like London. It doesn't.

In spring, worm guts boots watches

                                            pissy holes left by

dogs.

like Gena Rowlands the fight to live must make the kids notice
Mom. cross your ocean hope to die.
Mom transfers Bob to give her property municipally until her said
son reaches 35.
I take her inter-tropical suggestion: tear Levi-Strauss open to a
champagne send-off.

Dear Grandpa,
> *Ottawa is tighty whitey goosebumps bum.*
> *To keep warm, Mercutio shows me his Queen Maab.*
> *Mom forgot the mars-she-and-oh cherries in the*
> *sawine.*
> *We whistle while we work in space suits.*
> *38 cms.*
> *Deep snow!*

cucumber cabbage Sir Clifford Sifton kills the Indian summer
in my blue lagoon
grown-up Monte Cristo counts 52 villains in a deck of cards
joker Uncle Sultan searches coolie villages on hatched postcards
approach Guyana by peacock in the shadow of Olympus
dusting off Fazlah.

MOM & BOB: Matinees

*

Uncle Sultan: "See she with she Funk & Wagnall Sakatoon
berry jelly."

*

Mom'll bring Bob home in the dark.
Puppy, Dasher & Mouse: "Patois Patrols, if you see jumbie, bark!"
Frenchie the Watchman'll be asleep. & he'll wake up with
"Sorry, Mistress. I'll swim like Papillon.
I promise Devil's Island."

Shhhhh!quiet!

*

With Grandpa I see the Indian pictures,
Mom & Bob watch Peter Benchley
Jacqueline Bisset bubbles beneath & there's more sex in the books,
Mom cusses
& Nick Nolte's girlfriends run their lips up down this island
chalked on blackboards, she in him eye, these notes I take as I grow
outside dead Archie ab
into auntieman & now an American out with Bob, Mom dresses
like she looks good tonight
she will send her aura off with champagne, Gena Rowlands.

Deleted Scene

~~Mom drinks Bank's Beer, listens to Tim Maia.~~
~~gives rise to the~~
~~doublement soul~~

~~ref. to the Gothic~~
~~Massola (read him)~~
~~incognito not just any faggot~~
~~before we jerk off I reread Kant~~
~~last word last meal~~
~~ref. to Walpole queer scream~~
~~InHyoung, the hero, gives me a secular squeeze~~

~~cheers the battymen~~
~~open fly afternoon~~
~~Bruce Lee dungaree~~
~~corpse microphysique~~

~~Sister Brian says "Your father was a fullahman."~~
~~so I chase down "&s" speak in Bahasa~~

~~papayas mangoes many more red tapioca assalamwalaikumsand~~
~~sand sand earth like this before~~
~~"breathe"~~

BOYHOOD THINKS: Omnibus

0	"rice flour rotis? fuck off."
18 to 42	disco horizons —less that means never die pow! there's sex after, so saying, he caught up, and without wing or hippogriff, bore through the air over the wilderness and o'er the plain. read more hippogriff where the masters let them all hang out come on sons Daddy Night Mephistopheles bring the rubbers of course you and me, nuh?
29	Intermission Khatoon says, "I know we fond of comfort in the Savior. But we still cry. When they die we still cry. That little doubt in the comfort of the Savior." I says, "Huh?" Khatoon says, "You want some marzipan?"
6	*Hunt for Sweets*
plain	SEPTEMBER 13, _____	BY **KNEWS**	FILED UNDER **LETTERS**

Dear Editor,

On a purely utiliteaforthetillerman and theoreticull basis, the Feed the Nation campain was (what?) . Same goes for the PPP's updaytwo on the old model with its Grow More Food campaign. But such a consept sipping Cokes & playing games was badly (what?) executed by Burnham. The PPP's current campaign suffers from some of the frayaltease of Burnham's (what?) . Banning food first (don't-feel- good-like-a-steel-pan feelgood) then seeking to grow later is plain (what?) . Dictatorships don't make (what?) . (what?) of failed (what?) can result in (what?) starvation and

People eat several times every day. (what?) by wheat flour. Guyanese consumed anywhere from lbs of flour daily before the ban. Khatoon says this pan! Indians. Indians in Guyana really are Indias. not Amerindians how wide we grow wow wow pow

19   head griffin claws
            hooves horse tail
            Moors from Afrique?

37 to 43   disco with horizon means
            yes yes it does all end
            bump and grind bump and grind bump
            and grind
            like Mom & Bob you and me Canada izzan
            island berth death dearth
            birth like in Ray Harryhausen
            a thousand arms   Burnham was
                                           350,000 to 400,000
                                           done against

                                        Amerindians really
                                                    pow
hands everywhere
Sinbad, Sunday, 3pm
at Plaza

6 to 7   Mom put green aliens on the birthday cake
                   Mom poses mon chews wends thurs fry sat
                   sun morning downward dogs
                   at half past dinner
                   short pants time
                   little master
                   in panties

14   "the moonshine
                           the noontide sun
                           the work mine

                           a taste
                           of see
                           smell touch

                   OHMAMAMIA!MAMAMIA!"

15 to 18   Mittelholzer,
                   ever get sick slaves?
                   ever get sick servants?
                   ever hold shit in
                   on a sugar estate?

                       "don't spill the juice,
                                        Shabba!"

22

16	boy school high
	Prospero book drown
	I get
3 to 4	instant ego before hush hush shut
	up do it this way Mom in the gallery
	you can't always get what you want
	loud
	thinking
	"been here before atom bomb"
18 1/2	read more hippogriff mister
	half of her half of him, some Bob
	some Mom
41	skincareformendoiputaTMafterit?

in French bum hydramononcletante
that you left behind expires
scratchy shins now that Fall's starting,
no Soraksan,
can I still use it?
no noraebang & the mamamias mamamias
& after the Cass you
sing the high n' dry song
peacock balloon planet telex later
in a Seocho love motel
approaching
Pavonis Mons
I can see you jizz
jaw chin
baby's got the bends
blows loud balloons.

2.8 to 3.7	to be sung shortnin' shortnin' flung finger pointing at the moon "Hotei! Bring Archie back!"

46

the fact is queer I'm migration
if Guyana common denominator
for fuck off homophobe! If fuck off
homophobe begins
in Guyana on a scale of high-end to cheap
delicious,
how would I rate this Bakery 18 custard bun
I buy for a buck
at FRESHCO on Tecumseh
on a good day
see Detroit?

45 to 46

"time soon come/where Master plan slot/
the soul soon come"

12 to 14

just two
fish bowl
round round
Southampton Dock
the Windies

we making out boys got why girls
made out with boys

3

           staccato Don Giovanni
tongues turn bubblegum in fake stone,
drum roll, fanfare. *hey! that's my nightmare!*
Every funeral, a dress rehearsal,
at The Mikado
at the Savoy Theatre,

at Mom.

no ruku, sajjud. 4 takbirs, Sana Surah
Al-Fatiha, Mom: "oh yeah. I almost forgot
men want God to hear them first. Scunt!
That stinks." "Salat! Mom! Have respect!
Ba'ap said
in Saudi Arabia they'd flog you for that!"

Stand up! Darud! Yeah! Mom cries here. Mozart
begins a mouldy turn into Kaiso.
Archie, "and Muslims in general."
Hey! *That's my nightmare!* Every funeral, the 4th
takbir, remain standing,
say, "Salaam Archie:"

23 to 29	better than the hippogriff Kali comes to life behind Sinbad
0.2 to 45.9	in hybrid hands; Ottawa special effect. *"see, Orientalist!, see?"* ramsammy (fingersnap!) Albion (fingersnap!) puja Guyana (fingersnap!)
9	before Trudeau's fag-end Ottawa Greedo in the Old Somerset me & Bob, before our final morning in Georgetown & yesterday Mom sold the fridge, before I made this secret petition to Kali: "Give back Archie even in stone!"

Mom standing in the back
turns walaikum
into laughing Sparrow.

WAR CRIMINALS: Voice-over

(VO: yum drool yum drum roti & rum & yum drool yum drum roti & rum & yum drool yum drum)

InHyoung: What's roti?

      (& faster again & repeat again & again & "To All the Boys I've Loved After" & drool yum torch twang grew gay outside Guyana, eh? & Who cares about Ba'ap Mowsie? & Who cares about "wouldn't you like to be Guyana you?"

& Grew-Gay-Billy borrows Mittelholzer & Grew-Gay-InHyoung: "Wow! You look like Archie!" & "This is achar. My grandmother, Khatoon, makes it with tamarind. My mother's mother with tamarind."

      & the museums & Billy & InHyoung & like latkes & like panjeon & who I "love" more & where I "love" more & what the fuck? jean jacket leather skirt heels "...gotta do with it? ...gotta do with it? & yum drum Uncle Sultan was that rum-rotten coolie Mom warned me never to grow into &)

MOM & BOB: Matinees

*

as "art," as "poetics"

Wild Rose Manitoba no not a territory is Yukon one too? Prairie
Lily? Crocus? and yep in that order Dogwood Blue Violent
Mayflower Lady's Slipper I wait for the red man shush let him
blush in private OK? no Newfoundland White Lady Bob don't speak
as Fazlah asks bhai, which one is Trillium? How outside you grow?

*

If baby you're the bottom then I'm the sideways. Georgetown,
Guyana 1973. Do the Tower of Pisa. Do the Mona Lisa. Palm Court
Saturday Night. Spy Bob tops Mom, Mom tops Bob.

Bob: "In Canada, doughnuts. I promise."

*

The audience: Ba'ap, Mowsie, Archie, later Mom, later Bob,
sometimes forces "you too Mom you too
Mom" Khatoon too
    I practice Canada with cruise pansies Prince Albert Pelee
                                    Glacier.

Terror, of course, when Lady Auntieman get into Jack n' Jill dream
where I kiss two
time out for flapjacks.

MUSEUM: Outside Foreign

InHyoung, grow your hair long the muezzins call
the sun that obvious shine Ho & Lai head on shoulder
circle 10th in September to take a cab to the museum,
there'll be no rain we'd change the Wong Kar Wai
we'd miss the monsoon completely meet at the Door
to the Great Mosque in Cizre walk with the Rod of Moses
can you see me aching in another mid-afternoon Turkish delight?

(you will find him in a bowl of winged lions. Mazda,
that killing time, wrapped up in sweaty Calvins,
cruising park Ahabs)

limp before you find me in Composition X.
we don't want ajumma to hear your yuk yuk Classicists
in touch drunk nights
oh it's ok my chingu in the great escape button flys quick! quick!
behind the Kandinsky
you host
an evening of soju erotica.

(who sees Fuji from Tokyo I never did. let's get back
to Seoul.
please, not another jar from Peshawar,)

wear binoculars around your neck to dinner,
cross dress a neighbour.
Angie Dickinson standing by the Giacometti, Michael Caine always
in wigs.
before DVDS, you could find Push! Leolo! Push! on cassette
in Shindongnegori:
Montréal Gloria showing me how to heat up rice without a stove

                              spy on Etienne: wild carrot shirtless
sur le coin de Clark et St Viateur

(never walk with me in Yeouido regard the cherry blossoms;
hear ajoshi say some boys just wanna
                          spend money on Camaro penis cars.
not you I'll tell him.)

set fire to a Sir Walter Raleigh effigy in a car park.

(why does what makes the red man red hanamannadunga
feel so boyish? and, what's wrong
with the Rothko pu hup kkk ablaze
                          some orange up there some red down
                                                          here?)

no I don't cheat on you when I go to the museum.

                                          except that time

when I drank from the saucepan
of Abraham.

(your uncle was a tea farmer he would send us the best Sejak
from Halla. his friend Manu, the best from Tanah Rata.
there's this movie   where the actress gives the actor
                                  a blowjob would you like?
            Insadong cinematheque
                      & the intellegentsia gasp?)

                      all art remembers he turns tricks in Joseph's
                      turban

                                                                    29

Deleted Scene

~~"death's OK, Fazlah says. Paradise is better!"~~
~~yeah yeah since I was a kid this Roland Kirk talk to me every mon~~
~~chews wends thurs fry sat a sun days it's the same queen there~~
~~they'd say to me in 1939 Fazlah visits Germany with 60% reduction~~
~~in railroad fares British Subjects need no Visa just like here Gordon's~~
~~Gin comes from London, England there.~~

MUSEUM: Dance Floor

faggotguts gots
          spit   paradise garage phantasmagoric, Saint
flick prick
wand pretty, nuh?

"it was the lure of the big lights. Mephistopheles tunnels in the tubs
Saturnight's the best though surprised at Sunday afternoon's scorecard
fucking."

after stonewall this that
and fucking

spit: milky way hand hungry
            pays pays watch it and stand
            warm tug mouth son

                      imaginary got guts
                      lights! concrete! modern!

                              ("...tantrum in dad's yard
                              ("...disappointed on dancefloors
                              ("...on your knees whimsy skid

raleigh's guiana dabbles in alchemy
before london tower lock up spies far up the river
galileoscopes for spaniards.

Raleigh's guiana canoes fugitives upcountry
searches gold deposits fallen foul of his English expedition

few ornaments
twists NAMILCO cheese hope
"in sight of the great river
Orenoque."

                      pretty prick, nuh?

BOYHOOD THINKS: Jihaji Bhai

Latchmee sleeps on a Katya, a bed made out of knotted rope.

1983

> Bub
> shaved ice
> condensed milk
> sugar
> Mexico vanilla
> nutmeg
> limejuice sometimes

Mom says Khatoon likes it with rum. Mom's mom likes it
with rum & don't talk about Archie's mom.
Mowsie sticks scorpion peppers in your mouth. I'll tell you about
Latchmee is how Khatoon spells her
not Lakshmi light & stayed that way despite

a quake of fish & between India, Mauritius

make foamy with a Zulu Lulu

swizzle
stick

tuntun private parts laughs
Latchmee marries a Muslim doctor
there is no God except Allah

                                        coolies on the Hesperus

leaving Mauritius

                    for Demerara.

a glass of Bub.
Latchmee.
asleep on a *Katya*.

MOM & BOB: Matinees

oh yeah
find them plates

        on the wall air brush roses

                    kid!

         *

the genius of drinking straws is plaster of Paris listening
under her nails
soon, they'll be home. the 148'll pull up on Canterbury Ave.
Gilligan's Isle at 4. Mom'll laugh.
no ahir. no brahman. no chatri.
Calcutta. Natal. Demerara.
chop chop nostalgia.

my kid don't know the kind,

                 you know?

        *

this afternoon: burgers, fries, centuries serve no shakes.
sugar kills cities.

oh yeah

        *

cooliewoman

dogears
photobooks

                 kid!

God leave this suburb unlit
London shadow

            in winter

in my head not here

*

Bob said downtown Ottawa close its eyes dream of London.
It doesn't.

In spring, worm guts boots digs pissy holes left by dogs.
Wilkie Collins flips the bird at Mom's camera.

Georgetown jalousies
pining pine tarts.

Mom cries stories.

WAR CRIMINALS: Escape Roots

The night you woke up again
leaving Hebrew Academy in Cote St Luc someone assassinates you
again Art's mother never got Dachau scratch out she again
killed herself before he turned twelve these dreams of getting round up
murdered do you remember the dirty yous?
how Lauzon shows them?
that we kept far away from the French again.

That night I read Edgar's bone flute he could hear French &
German & English & Italian but the tongues
he could not identify "too deaf ear to describe" that made
the Kit Kat a swastika & a frozen end & a song & a dance dead cabaret
Sally Bowles faraway how push Leolo push echoes
through an empty bus station as Christopher Isherwood
backs back into Britain can you see that?
& the cloak and dagger coating his cock those boys still swimming
bad hard bags along the Rhine Moselle Mosul in California
he'd resurrect wilkommen bring the music play back
to the fag ends.

Edgar spent a year here before the cold drove him back to Guyana
he wrote "a degree of negro parentage"
in a cafe he told me "I am an offshoot" he told
"I am an offshoot of a Swiss-German plantation manager
of the 18th century of a Frenchman from Martinique
of an Englishman from Lancashire" but that little black in me
used to live somewhere near here maybe next door
to Bains Coloniale? Next door to the Family Robinsons?

We'd swim bear hug the dream pull our trunks down at La Cite
bienvenue low culture stoned

can you hear the drums
Fernando listens even to Portuguese love songs next door
bem vinda in drag where the orchestra leaves
your troubles at the door
Pirate Jenny's shoot-em-ups piled higher and higher
in the "that'll learn ya!" countdown escape routes
the Indians like the Jews Steve McQueen root root escape
Uncle Sultan even got his mistress out
tell me again about Baumgartner through Bombay into Venice.

Deleted Scene

~~Erect Cinema L'Amour beefcake~~

~~genealogies~~

~~my body on the other side Mephistopheles at midnight,~~
~~a "Modern Soul" wow!~~

~~Canada izzan island~~

~~did you say that?~~
~~that~~

MOM & BOB: Matinees

- ✓ Je viendrai courir pour attacher vos souliers.
- ✓ don't forget the punk rock bop at the end.
- ✓ you don't recognize me, huh, Guyanaizzan
- ✓ an island? Mom says.
- ✓ & I've come home
- ✓ Robin Hood rotis
- ✓ avec guitars & Veronica Lake hair
- ✓ & Fazlah asks, "Do you speak French?"
- ✓ I speak cartoon Khatoon bumper car cartoon
- ✓ not humpy
- ✓ not dumpy
- ✓ dumbtea
- ✓ ahjee for Archie's ma
- ✓ what? for Khatoon?
- ✓ "That's Bob with 1-oh!"
- ✓ Fernando drums
- ✓ Sleep
- ✓
- ✓ don't call her that, Mom says
- ✓ bumper car tea tea
- ✓ Tang's cake box
- ✓ dumpt
- ✓ humpt

WAR CRIMINALS: 4575 Henri-Julien

in the wrong place above Fernando's because
I saw this film once *[jeez why didn't I ever fuck a side of beef?*
I heard "I Just Wanna Know" slow jams radio to stop
those nights in Montréal
here, Bob brought Mom for le super-sexe Olympic Aida
St Denis sup]
or here, Ven brought me for the in-those-days-Moroccan-not-
cheap-Afghani-shit
in those days, Pirate Jenny smoke some dance some
"that'll learn ya!" Manhattans in the dyke bar away from the men's
let's just kiss and say goodbye
[jeez I never got to say goodbye Auntieman Lady found a letter
you wrote me
on the radio, after Reagan, and Lou was right there were no
parades
on Halloween] or
humid goodbye writes was I ever equatorial? I ain't got no
believe you.
Iqbal was a ball motorcycle Pride Punjabi comb,
right tight? *[jeez I saw this play once where Billy kept saying gay*
without pets. Goldbloem Bogo racing through the apartment
Henri-Julien, why here? Why not a little farther up where
they speak English?]
or drunk yes drunk we'd walk up Duluth screaming
push! Leolo! push! before hitting The Main, the hippies come out
the hippies come out in springtime *[jeez there I'd go, open mad*
unlock the ancestors, hear them:
we've found you! we've found you!] or
I once read this book everyone became hypertelic
hard words I looked them up click click view them exceed passage

dem get to die
on dry land water what water? Crusoe used up Caliban
not again paradime *[jeez and me*
here trying this tongue like Cesaire like with all that sand?
in the wee wee we
could scream the archipelago push bhai push squeeze your way
out dash
the yourope equals Aziz collar back stud to Fielding] or
there was Billy beside ourselves, again belly floats
don't wake Fernando oats snoring down
can you hear the drum
sticks on stairs?

MUSEUM: Cinerama

& consider these follow-up fashion stories blood upon
   your Osama bin Laden shoulder
& the way we listen to Barrington Levy in Montréal, right Billy?
& not stroking a Persian not wanting SPECTRE SMERSH
& Taliban don't rhyme
& no Gershwin skyscraper eavesdrops on the Garvey I carry
   back pocket
& from Medan to Maninjaw, "you must try Padang food!"
& Duluth above Fernando Mile End too far Feb. -44 this evening
& I don't give a damsel about hockey.
& In Banda Aceh I rhyme Bahasa Guyanese
& sila buka bibiru kasut have some cashews before you leave
& "OK, Old Village?"
& Guyana izzan an island in Java you know?
& He swallowed Pavonis Mons with his shuttle. Early afternoon.
& I found Kananga in St Ann Yaphet Koto Arawaki adze
& (the kids laugh when I say, "Not Canada. Not Canada.")
& When I see his face, a Taliban tee.
& and no jumbie spoke to me no Sarawak spook not Spanish X
   not French X not Pourtagee X
& Don't Know What theremin dragonflies
   above the Forbidden City
& that's what's closing
& the ushers call me "Sir Sir it's time to leave the museum"
& the five minutes palace in the Tuesday price Pu Yi's red doors
& in out into hi hello hallow head belly full
& Roger Moore's audio guide to the Palace Museum
& ECHO Roger Moore's audio guide to the Palace Museum
& Vincent Van Ven muscular alley planks
   stubborn to Attack of the Wood Ants! called

& I sang Demerara Groenhart's "O lime bush ripe."

& Neapolitan-lush like Caruso, thank you please come again,
    drink cloves & milk in Kalibaru.

& hitch a ride from Jogja to Bromo dragonfly kite rucksack luck

& But this is Sarawak & Don't Know What's talking to me.

& Not Fazlah long arm leg rest in Berbice chair,

& Not Mom, Muskoka chair, me & Bob & leeches at Meech Lake

& Jay Scott dyes a draft dodger Adirondak in Toronto.

& "Draw white light like Ba'ap in ihram bust through
    the back door

& circle my bed "been around the world and I can't find my baby
    and I and I" don't hope to die

& force-field against night fest toons Pa's Americas
    a Cast of Characters KAPOWS!

& yardstick, wooden with silver ends,
    "you from outside now, bhai!" it's not the end of the world

& don't arkestra know that yet Sun Ra?"

& earshot Mohammedan measures says no know Kolkata
    to the peek-a-boo prince hard

& as I wash my ass 100% cotton, made in India,
    forgive me money belt, five thousand Riyals,

& Don't eat with the left.

& "Cultural relics are irretrievable/Please be careful
    when viewing them"

& In the Pavilion of Prolonged Sunshine, finger food history,
    Archie's calligraphy.

& (he) real like earth (swarthy) real like dirt

& yeah yeah in "The age-old and splendid historical civilization
    of the Chinese Nation" my heart wanked

& Satan right-handed chauffeured car rental
    Jakarta trapped in Chagall's red city

& "surely, we can be gay here? sweet & handsome?"

& In Montréal, Ven drops by every Sunday every

"So, what the war said this week master?" greeting.

& We Parliament Hill the headlines

& high high high Lost Horizon Everest in the "that'll learn ya!"

& Nina defecating, as Lauryn sang, on the microphone.

& Cook-up now "all a we" or how Bob loved Mom creolized.

& In the deck of cards, 52 terrorists, I found Faz, Abdel, Sultan
cha cha.

& No women yet.

& Holy Shit! Dragonfly! Sleeping Palace. I blame it. I blame it.
On midnight.

& Did these kids who lose a cricket ball in a compound
know they mouth mouth with a father like mine?

& Real coolieman nacion natio flips the bird in nations like mine

& "So, what the war said?" Ven spooning dhall
from Khatoon's recipe into the Royal Doulton bowl.

& You see? The we split we split ships chips against rock
Limoges wrapped in newspaper

& Mom, Bob, Mowsie, Ba'ap & Jay Scott says William Wyler it
"lemme tell you some kiss,"

& yell like those same kids I met in Java sir! sir!
postcard? postcard? Osama's poking proud faded tees

& nose eye Taliban piece Gregory Peck's *Rome. By all means, Rome*
on his head

& I don't want anything, I don't want anything. Just to see
the Buddha's mouth open Yankie.

& Before Jogja, in Banda Aceh I heard Ven fi true Halloween

& the screaming God in the Grand Mosque, the djinns
in the marble that kept the wave away

& spared Hassan

& Mom ate Thalidomide in Wales to profit in language.

BOYHOOD THINKS: Mecca to Madina, 2009

if Ba'ap jump out boo! how can you do Umrah,
nasty mind?

AND

Zubeda says, if you get nervous, if you forget what to do,
look at the other pilgrims. do what they do.
& when you first see the Kaaba,
put your wish hard into Abraham. He'll listen.

AND

ladadiladada ladadiladada ladadiladada ladadiladada ladadiladada
sing for Cairo throwing thrones a prince hip a swollen lip
leave your *somethingsomethingsomethingsomethingsomething*
somethingsomethingsomething at the door
say safety pins
hold up ihram
bang bang

AND

forgive memoneybelt   forgive memoneybelt   forgive belt

AND

stegosaurus suck
as pilgrims walked in circles kissing stone
I gave thanks for you,

your cock too

AND

pissing in the desert's not the same as pissing in the snow
you can't know yellow white melt sunken grey dancehalls
full of noughts

AND

Scatter!
yana   hey yanoho   gu ya na guy ana guya na
g u y a n a   heyyanaho   guy
wait for Ba'ap to ok bhai,
what you do with the i-a-n-a?
Walter Scott in Twyfords toilet bowl
yeah bhai!
and me submitted
through
spilt
we split we split ran down the road with some sweet handsome
porky soft bat face bwoy

Deleted Scene

~~Tomorrow, leave for Mecca Madina.~~
~~"Just don't let them see you reading the Mittelholzer~~
~~instead of the Pickthall.~~
~~That's bad enough but even the Egyptians on the bus~~
~~won't go for that.~~
~~The fake word of God is better~~
~~than all that witchcraft."~~
~~I brush my teeth with a Miswak.~~
~~I am alone in an ocean.~~
~~Jizzin' djinnee izza Canada island wonder.~~

WAR CRIMINALS: Beefcake

: "my uncle a tea farmer the best from Shizouka"
: "Glenlivet in jeans disco much?"
: "B movie brain eaters at the Mun Hwa Sauna"
: "on a clear day we could see Fuji from Tokyo"
: "young people spend their money on cars"
: "yabazabbah77 a stoic cummer before the 6 a.m. to Pusan"
: "mazurkas in the morning fucking around"
: "glory hole mouth"
: "sci-fi soju tongue slow down"
: "cufflinks straddle elephants la dadi la dada"
: "conquistador, pull thy root!"
: "wild combos"
: "fought in Phuket before salat again"
: "sipping cocks and playing games"
: "such big hands Richard Carlson potato queens"
: "like Choi jin-sil if they catch Leslie Cheung in my mouth"
: "curious Osan tonight"
: "feed your buddy nuts"
: "or d'oeuvre huts introduce my pigs in a blanket"
: "sweaty Calvins cruising"
: "through the gloryhole runtime 14:58"
: "coxswain blades the first boy I ever just call me Flop"
: "a long time ago Lake Ontario rusty padlocks"
: "I'm the top. I'm Napoleon brandy."
: "PictouAndrewViewedYou5MinutesAgo"
: "without hats, bugger here"
: "POZ cuz"
: "days of being wild like Andy Lau"
: "cum eater class struggle feedin"
: "rimjob $$$"

: "Canada izzan island"
: "ice cream balloons"
: "dutty choon"
: "when kaka hole is laHffing lolli …la la la la anything goes"
: "muscle toy milk"

MOM & BOB: Matinees

*

Mowsie
ahjee
cough
up
drops
Strepsils
pocket

*

by Night big letter here cause it's a character, old black magic
Night you lock out, spits
Awar, Dasim, Sut, and Tir from its palms, Ali Baba Ali Baba,
coughs up Mowsie, blood love blood love,
she is
Archie's mum, she'll drag the bodies of the kids away.

*

Mowsie shows up in the Antonioni psych trip Mom is having
in the living room. I smell
zeb grass Tea
for the Tillerman background.

*

When
Mowsie shows,
snapsnappaddywhack

take Archie away cry so hard for him Heaven spill over
get chased by wood ants
so hard I look like Archie

                                                    Mom
                                                   locks
                                                 Mowsie
                                                     out

Bob
laughs.

MUSEUM: Close-ups

Archie:

Mom: "I already know the terror of holidays. I have already buried you."

Archie:

Ba'ap: "Don't play in the masjids after dark."

Archie:

Ba'ap:

Uncle Sultan: "I cut my hair to look more like a boy in Fazlah's abstract God."

Khatoon: "Omit the unspeakable vice of the Greeks in Uncle Sultan."

Archie:

Uncle Sultan: "The Dutch will fuck their way through my wild blood."

Archie.

Uncle Sultan: "Alone with Jan Michael Vincent at the Metropole. The colonies flicker."

Archie:

Mom: "Bob appears. The real America winks at me."

Archie:

Mom:

Uncle Sultan:

Mom: "Bob is a handsome killer. Suave thriller. Tidal wave hurricane flood. He hooks me."

Archie:

Bob: "My mother runs a comb through my dead-straight European hair."

Archie:

Archie:

Khatoon: "My eyes roll through jalousies out/into New Amsterdam."

Mowsie: "Kaffirs line up outside the slaughterhouse for black pudding blood."

Khatoon: "We split wide long ago you know?"

Fazlah: "A rotted teeth Hindu sits beside me."

Mowsie: "They smell like second-class cow dung."

Archie:

Mom: "Sometimes Demerara Radio speaks of women who blow themselves up Battle of Algiers."

Ba'ap:

Mom: "I keep postcards that say East Indian types typical coolie upper Canada spins around."

Archie:

BOYHOOD THINKS: 15 Movies in 15 Seconds

& cuatro Crimes and Misdemeanours

& brownies we never made.

& 21 rue Fleureuse laughs at Peter Sellers, right?

& Fernando sleeps I love you still like Alice bee toke.

& we never made Crimes & Misdemeanours laugh at Gertrude's
    brownies

& Merry Christmas, Mr Lawrence Tom Conti breaks Bowie's heart

& Ryuichi Sakamoto also and the drip from the tip David Sylvian
    yes him

& Night of the Living Dead when we should've been in front of the
    TV

& but who the fuck was Di die? Billy said crashing in the same car

& Star Wars I'd say that was Mom

& "Crying is cleansing." (Dionne Warwick)

& Mom prays behind the men at the Rafeek Mosque it's just as
    well she'd say

& they all fart when they lean over smash their heads spot on God,
    see?

& yes Billy Star Wars ruined Hollywood but it's 1977 & this is
    Ottawa & Destination Moon

& still here 8 1/2 Mowsie in the kitchen cooking Ba'ap big pop in
    the masjid plotting pipes

& cherry tobacco that's right I smell Grandpa

& I wish Mom could watch the end of Full Metal Jacket Hanoi in
    the eyes of the sniper

& the only woman in the film is All About My Mother because it
    comes out the year Mom dies

& before she gives me Truman Capote's show in the Europa, Europa
    Cabaret finales

& this freedom to show our cut cocks right, brother? cross Dresden again freedom to be semite

& Muslim semite Jew Marmite at the garden parties of the Finzi-
Continis

& I still write her like in Farewell, Children Jean Patou in the hotels
of her white letters

& Mom's Empire of the Sun bomb middle-class bridge bring
bandits out to play in fly-away feet that pines

& I am in sea mud Alta Vista trudge no catfish on Canterbury Ave

& *I learned a new word today* Rajastaniniatombomb

& I am a faggot Tom Finland who dreams a fetish fest these are my
Querelle paper men lime

& Georgetown Sew Wall from Camp Street to Kitty

Deleted Scene

~~cruise poesie~~
~~erect theatre~~
~~impossible-Guyana ribald bullfrog-in-the-dungarees~~

~~Fazlah's library izzan island~~

~~I am not the son of God~~

~~Perfumed-Garden rattlesnakes~~
~~Alcazar shoots genip seeds at my feet~~
~~are me "gonna take you higher"?~~
~~all this Hergé porno~~
~~Harold Robbins army? arm-y.~~

~~Sir Walter Raleigh laughs.~~
~~Come clean me up!~~

MOM & BOB: Matinees

*

-27
the moon settles down with a man in

star
gaze
bhai
super
nova
monkey
mountain
Paka
Raima

*

"I am searching Archie's expiry date."

Kolkata
gargles
Bob
marzipan
Mom

"Khatoon says Potaro-Siparuni's haunted."

*

Mom's toes mix with sand Bob's toes wait with

MUSEUM: Schlock

on warm evenings while walking in the footprints of PBUH
he who will not be named PBUH, just in case, when I went on
                                        Umrah
there was this prayer for you in your bent chest & with iron nails
fixed to dragons in central Anatolia
                    I cut my hair between Safa and Marwah.

            (when we crossed the Han River the running family
            without Richard Dawson
            Gwoemul in the film in my brain
            listen to it the sound of my piss wizzzzzzzzerd
            the river so full of my wizzzard)

break the pink hearts apart waterfalls the coo coo roo coo coo
                                never shared with you
all these hearts in front of the beaux arts? once, Bahram IV had this
                                        dagger
I walked thousands of years into the past

who wiped you clean at night? was it the king
in the spirit of all those queens on Homo Hill that made
you ceremonial?

(I resisted his necklaces in agate glass gold Carnelian,
matched the Portuguese Dutch English
Japan a Staebrok Market in Melaka scarlet; fleets of UFOs
above Fukishima, look!

born in Georgetown.)

ever "approach Pavonis Mons by balloon"
            send more   pictures

                    earthquakes great winds fires famine

you think Chagall the only peacock in all those mountains
make me dusty this elaborate passport lie
we only slowly grew west I keep postcards that say East Indian
typical coolie village upper Canada chingu the world
spins around you

(are you a student of history he asks which no one asks in Seoul
this insertion into the English Gatekeeper sexy, I declare
no poet of Sycorax scratches the part in his hair, not just another
                              eye drop   you   in   the   ocean)

BOYHOOD THINKS: Best Original Score

a cassava lie: check your catch
& the-mamas-and-the-papas-you're-driving-your-children-insane
end credits.
curtain close: Kaiteur tears.
rhetorical flourish: *let me tell you about the Pops,*
these LPs were tropical once.
Bob to Caliban: what are these LPs doing in Khatoon's roasted
breadfruit?
the bacchanal threat in minimalist disco:
"I came for the ass. Wait. What?"
this part must make Fazlah dance 70s & 80s: house arrest
contraband cha cha cha
& the yrs: & don't snap your fingers in the Visitors line & don't
search Mom's Samsonite for extra
Colgate, *please, don't snap my fingers, chew hubba hubba, act the*
fool fool white boys I lime with.
don't let them search that suitcase. OK, ole higue?"

WAR CRIMINALS: End Credits

                                                    Saturday night

                                                          pound
                                                          street
                                                           cake
                                                          scarf
                                                           tied
          "les quartre cent coups"/i thought i heard you say
                                                          right?
                  it's always some boy Genet will want to fuck
                             in ten years or so
                         shelved at Boite Noire
                         as the French New Wave
                                                          right?
          "goodbye fucking children"/even Louis Malle shows up
                          Luftwaffe mouth
                          that's some shit
                          I cried for hours
                        lights out lights up

Let's go to Infidels
feed truffles to Truffaut
six pack eight pack
hot stuff,
eh?

                                                            fag
                                                           guts

                  e trip avec avec avec up
                  to so long Marianne
                          6 a.m. eternal

-27

swamped
butt

spin
spin
sugar
soft

-ed

Franken
fish

-ended

the fags
Bob Fosse moves

Song
&
Cancer dance

friends in faded brown cords
nut huggers on the 55 St Laurent
"I wanna see all my friends at once/ I wanna go bang"/back
couldn't wait to wake Fernando up
wouldn't you like to be Guyana you?
be Guyana be be Guyana

rough
thumb
monster

hitch rides
bleu nuit train

galaxy
dungarees

glory
hole knees

Acknowledgements

While the stories, names, characters, and incidents appearing in *The Greatest Films* are fictitious, the films and music I repurpose for the poems are real.

Here are partial lists of the main filmic and sonic sources found in the text:

The Films:

Jane Eyre (1943, Stevenson)
The Train (1970, Nagaich)
Last Tango in Paris (1972, Bertolucci)
High Noon (1952, Zinnemann)
Peter Pan (1953, Geronimi, Jackson, Luske, Kinney)
Empire of the Sun (1987, Spielberg)
Happy Together (1997, Kar-wai)
Clash of the Titans (1981, Davis)
The Other Side of Midnight (1977, Jarrott)
The Way We Were (1973, Pollack)
Hamlet (1948, Olivier)
A Streetcar Named Desire (1951, Kazan)
Maurice (1987, Ivory)
The Land That Time Forgot (1975, Connor)
Au Revoir Les Enfants (1987, Malle)
The Great Escape (1963, Sturges)
The Poseidon Adventure (1972, Neame)
Doctor Zhivago (1965, Lean)
Europa, Europa (1990, Holland)
Woman Under the Influence (1974, Cassavetes)
Romeo and Juliet (1936, Cukor)
Snow White and the Seven Dwarfs (1939, Hand, Jackson, Morey, Sharpsteen, Cottrell, Pearce)

The Deep (1977, Peter Yates)
The Golden Voyage of Sinbad (1974, Hessler)
Prospero's Books (1991, Greenaway)
Dressed to Kill (1980, De Palma)
Léolo (1992, Lauzon)
Gwoemul (2006, Bong Joon-ho)
Cabaret (1972, Fosse)
A Passage to India (1984, Lean)
Live and Let Die (1973, Hamilton)
The Last Emperor (1987, Bertolucci)
Roman Holiday (1953, Wyler)
Lost Horizon (1937, Capra)
Creature from the Black Lagoon (1954, Arnold)
Days of Being Wild (1990, Kar-wai)
Battle of Algiers (1966, Pontecorvo)
Shadow of the Hawk (1976, McCowan)
I Love You, Alice B Toklas (1968, Averback)
Crimes and Misdemeanours (1989, Allen)
Merry Christmas, Mr Lawrence (1983, Oshima)
Night of the Living Dead (1968, Romero)
Querelle (1982, Fassbinder)
Full Metal Jacket (1987, Kubrick)
All About My Mother (1999, Almodóvar)
Star Wars (1977, Lucas)
Frogs (1972, McCowan)
The Running Man (1987, Glaser)
The 400 Blows (1959, Truffaut)

The Music:

"Warm Leatherette," The Natural
"Chaiyya Re Chaiyya Re," Asha Bhosle
"Cucurrucucú Paloma," Caetano Veloso
"Thorn of Crowns," Echo & The Bunnymen
"My Funny Valentine," Shirley Bassey

"Nani Wine," Crazy

"Oye Como Va," Tito Puente & His Orchestra

"Adolf Hitler," Clifford Morris (Mighty Destroyer)

"Approaching Pavonis Mons by Balloon," The Flaming Lips

"Loving You,"Minnie Ripperton

"Zombie," Fela Kuti

"Whistle While You Work," Adriana Caselotti

"Bohemian Rhapsody," Queen

"Mr Loverman," Shabba Ranks

"The Bends," Radiohead

"Wish You Were Here," Pink Floyd

"You're the Top," Ella Fitzgerald

"Disappointed on Dancefloors," Metronymy

"Fireworks," The Tragically Hip

"Pirate Jenny," Nina Simone

"Ain't Got No," Nina Simone

"Gypsy Woman," Crystal Waters

"Ceremony," New Order

"Ready or Not," Fugees

"Tea for the Tillerman," Cat Stevens

"Go Bang," Dinosaur L (Arthur Russell)

These poems were made possible by the support, love, eyes, and edits of many wonderful people. But, most of all, I must thank Andre, Amanda, Carol, Cheran, Gaiutra, Helena, Karin, Kofi, Louis, Melanie, LZ, Luna, Nicole, NourbeSe, Anurima, Samantha, Shivaun, Susan, Rajiv, Ramona, Richard, & Rob.

Special love to John, Julian, Zalina, & Shelly.

To Mawenzi House for always taking risks and for welcoming me into their family.

To the ancestors, the best ghosts in the world.

To the familiar spirit by my side in the shape of a dog, Sabrina.